the LITTLE BOOK of
empathy

the LITTLE BOOK of
empathy

enrich your life
through compassion
and kindness

kirsten riddle

CICO BOOKS
LONDON NEW YORK

Published in 2022 by CICO Books
An imprint of Ryland Peters & Small Ltd
20–21 Jockey's Fields   341 E 116th St
London WC1R 4BW   New York, NY 10029
www.rylandpeters.com

10 9 8 7 6 5 4 3 2 1

Text © Alison Davies 2022
Design © CICO Books 2022
For picture credits, see page 144.

A CIP catalog record for this book is available from the Library of Congress
and the British Library.

ISBN: 978-1-80065-018-3

Printed in China

Designer: Fahema Khanam
Commissioning editor: Kristine Pidkameny
Senior commissioning editor: Carmel Edmonds
Art director: Sally Powell
Creative director: Leslie Harrington
Production manager: Gordana Simakovic
Publishing manager: Penny Craig
Publisher: Cindy Richards

contents

introduction

Empathy is universal. It is the unseen thread that connects every living thing upon the earth, the artist's brush that deftly brings out the color of the picture; empathy makes things real. There is no rhyme or reason to it, no sense of order. It is something that ebbs and flows within us and can rise to the surface at any moment. To feel true empathy is a gift, even when it brings pain and suffering to the heart. It allows us to make deeper connections with others and build bridges. It is the salve of understanding and the elixir of hope, for both giver and receiver. It means, even in your darkest hour, you are not alone.

When you practice empathy, you step into the shoes of someone else and walk in their skin. You feel what they feel, see what they see, and know instinctively what they are going through. Empathy is raw. It is not something you can do at arm's length. Instead, you must cast aside your guard, open your heart, and let the magic happen. While it is not for the risk-averse, it is rewarding. It brings light and love into your life, and when it becomes second nature, you'll notice it spreading further afield, connecting you to your community and the wider world.

Could a greater miracle take place than for us to look through each other's eyes for an instant?

Henry David Thoreau (1817–1862)

Empathy is a choice, and just like any decision it takes courage and conviction, but once made, it is an easy path to follow. All you have to do is tap into the feeling, and let it wash over you. The fact you have this book in your hands is the first step. In these pages, you will find a compendium of insights, facts, tips, and techniques to help you on your journey. As well as the different types of empathy and how it works, you will learn about your true empathic nature, what an empath is, and what to do if you think you are one. You will also become aware of empathy at large in your community, environment, and relationships. Whether you want to connect more with others, take a mindful approach to caring, or simply open your heart and feel the love, this little guide will help.

Engage, enjoy, and be empathic!

CHAPTER 1

what is empathy?

defining empathy

Empathy is about sharing someone else's pain, experiencing their vulnerability, and allowing yourself to not only feel what they are feeling, but also to see things from their perspective. Over the years, science has discovered that when we witness an event that might cause distress to others, it triggers the parts of the brain that deal with the action and experience of feeling emotions. In other words, we feel and act as if it is happening to us. We mirror the experience in our mind, and "catch" the same emotions, which then creates a need in us to do something to ease the other person's pain. Some people feel more deeply than others and find it easier to connect with people at this level, but we all have the ability to empathize.

empathy vs compassion

Compassion and sympathy are related to empathy, but just like cousins on a family tree, they are distinctly different in the way they work. When we empathize with someone, we actively put ourselves in their shoes and experience the same emotions. When we have compassion for someone, we recognize what they are going through and find ways to show we care. When we sympathize, we feel sorry for what the person is going through and find ways to make this known, even though we do not share their feelings. This connection is passive, rather than proactive, and doesn't always result in us doing something to ease the other person's suffering.

Empathy: the ability to share and understand the feelings of another.

Empathy is seeing with the eyes of another, listening with the ears of another, and feeling with the heart of another.

Alfred Adler (1870–1937)

types of empathy

Empathy is not a one-size-fits-all concept. There are three main types of empathy that you can experience, depending on the type of person you are and the situation.

affective empathy

Also known as emotional empathy, this is about understanding and sharing what the other person is feeling. For example, you might see someone suffering heartache, and actually feel a pain within your heart as you go through the same emotions. When you experience affective empathy, you sense, feel, and understand at a heart level.

cognitive empathy

This type of empathy is about understanding what is going on in the mind and how a person is thinking. It can help us connect and communicate more effectively with others, because we understand what resonates with them at a deeper level. We connect with their mental state and imagine what they are thinking. When you show cognitive empathy, you can easily see things from another person's perspective.

compassionate empathy

This takes empathy to the next stage: not only do we think and feel what the other person is going through, but we are also moved to take action and alleviate their suffering in whatever way we can. We reach out, connect, and do our best to make the person feel better.

BE EMPATHIC: everyday empathy

Every day we are presented with opportunities to exercise empathy. Whenever you interact with someone, ask yourself, "How can I be more empathic?" Make a point of having one empathic encounter each day where you pause and think about what you're going to say. Ask what is on the person's mind and how they are feeling, then listen and digest their response. It might not come naturally at first, but asking those questions in your head, and then out loud, will help you develop these skills, until eventually you'll do it without thinking.

When people talk, listen completely.
Most people never listen.

Ernest Hemingway (1899–1961)

what kind of empathy works for you?

You are unique. You have your own talents and skill set, your likes and dislikes, and all those special gifts and quirks that make you awesome, so it makes sense you'll have your own empathy style.

Whether you are a natural at tuning in to how someone feels, or the kind of person that prefers to think with their head, and figure out what's on someone's mind, you'll have a way of approaching empathy and making it work for you. This mini quiz will help you identify your empathic style, and once you know where your natural gifts lie, you'll be able to make the most of them. Answer the questions honestly and tot up the number of As, Bs, and Cs at the end, then read the results on pages 20–21 to discover what kind of empathy works for you.

1. Your best friend is in floods of tears because she has split from her partner. What do you do?

a) I feel heartbroken for her and give her a big hug and a shoulder to cry on.

b) I can imagine what she must be thinking and offer some comforting words.

c) I make her a drink and sit down with her, and we talk it through until she feels better.

2. You have just watched a movie which ends in tragedy. How do you feel?

a) You are an emotional wreck and have run out of tissues.

b) You cannot stop picturing the final scene and thinking about what happened.

c) You're upset so you go for a walk to lift your spirits.

3. Two of your work colleagues are having
a disagreement and it is getting heated.
How do you cope?

a) You get stressed and on edge.

b) You can imagine what they are both thinking
and see both sides.

c) You step in and act as mediator to solve the problem.

4. You're sitting next to a lady on the bus and she
starts to cry. What do you do?

a) You feel upset for her and do your best
to console her.

b) You try and imagine what has caused her distress.

c) You talk to her gently and ask what you
can do to help.

5. A stray cat has turned up on your doorstep and it looks like it is injured. What do you do?

a) You sense where it is hurting and feel upset for the poor thing.

b) You try and picture how it got the injury in the first place.

c) You do your best to keep the cat calm and ring a vet or animal charity.

quiz results

mostly As: your empathy style is **emotional**

You are a sensitive soul, who feels things very deeply. You do not have to try and sense how someone is feeling as it comes naturally to you, and you often find yourself overwhelmed by the emotions of others. Your caring nature means you're always on hand in a crisis. Sensitive to moods and atmospheres, you need to learn how to protect yourself from absorbing too much negativity.

mostly Bs: your empathy style is **cognitive**

Your mind is always active, and you find it easy to see and understand what others are thinking. Your ability to put yourself in the mindset of others means you are great at communicating and getting your message across. You know how people think and find it easy to connect with them. You tend to read situations quickly and know just what to say to make things better.

mostly Cs: your empathy style
is **compassionate**

You are a practical person with a heart of gold. For you,
it's all about solutions, so when you see someone in
need, you'll do your best to help in any way you can.
Your objective nature means you'll be able to weigh up
both sides of an argument and see a way forward.
Proactive and caring, you combine thought and emotion,
and then take positive action.

I USE MY OWN
UNIQUE GIFTS TO
REACH OUT
TO OTHERS.

Yet, taught by time, my heart has learned to glow for other's good, and melt at other's woe.

Homer (c. 800 BCE–c. 701 BCE)

be, share, feel...

When someone is empathic, they are sensitive
to what is going on around them. They feel at
a much deeper level, taking on the pain of others
and internalizing it. The thoughts and emotions they
experience are genuine and heartfelt. It's not about
pity, but about being, sharing, and feeling.

I share,
I feel,
I am aware.

TRY THIS:

listen, relate, equate

Affective empathy goes to the heart of the matter and deals with feelings at their purest and rawest level. If you want to build emotional empathy, you have to be prepared to go deep. To really feel what someone else is going through you need to listen, relate, and equate.

- **LISTEN** to what the other person is telling you. Let them share how they feel, and don't interrupt, whether that's to sympathize or tell them you've been in a similar situation. Remember this is about the other person opening up, and you fully "hearing" what they have to say.

- **RELATE** to what you have heard. Take a moment to imagine how they feel. Think of a time when you felt the same emotion and take yourself back to that moment.

- **EQUATE** what they are feeling with what you have felt in the past. Connect the emotion and feel it in your heart.

build cognitive empathy

One of the easiest ways to build cognitive empathy is to spend time getting to know lots of different people. Learn as much as you can about them. Look at their facial expression and body language—what does it tell you about what they are feeling? Ask questions and check if you are right in your assumptions. The more you ask and learn, the more you'll get to know how different people think.

remember

It doesn't matter how much you want to empathize with another person, there will always be times when it does not work, when you miss the mark, and you're unable to connect. This is not a failure. We all go through tough times, and we deal with it differently. At any one moment we experience a range of emotions, and so it can be hard for others to put themselves in our position and feel what we are truly feeling. Emotional stress surfaces in various ways, and everyone has their own strategy for coping. Some people put up a wall and do their best not to let others in, and some people put on an act and pretend it is not happening. There is no right or wrong way, and as long as your intentions are good and you are striving to empathize, you are doing all you can to make the world a better place.

BE EMPATHIC: checking in

Being in tune with your emotions is an important part of empathy, and this starts with you and what you are feeling. Be true to yourself and acknowledge how you feel throughout the day.

• Spend a couple of minutes at the beginning and the end of every day just gazing at your reflection in the mirror.

• Make eye contact and hold your gaze.

• Ask yourself, "How am I feeling right now?"

• Take note of your expression and the way you are holding yourself and acknowledge whatever emotion rises to the surface.

• Say, "I engage with my emotions and embrace who I am and what I am feeling right now."

Checking in with yourself regularly will give you a sense of where you are in your life and help you open up and release any emotions that are weighing you down.

Male vs. female

"I feel your pain" is a popular phrase that is used in society to show we care, but while we all like to think that we can empathize with each other, who does it more, men or women? And does gender affect how much you empathize with others?

According to a study by Leonardo Christov-Moore, a UCLA postdoctoral fellow in psychiatry and biobehavioral sciences, and Dr. Marco Iacoboni, a director at the UCLA Ahmanson-Lovelace Brain Mapping Center, women are better than men at feeling the pain of others. They studied brain imagery, taken by MRI, when a group of people were exposed to a video clip which showed a hand being poked by a syringe. The purpose was to measure the immediate reflexes and neural responses in the brain on seeing someone else in pain. They looked at blood oxygen levels and changes in blood flow to determine how much participants engaged with the image. The results showed that the females of the group showed a higher reaction in the area of the brain that mimics the pain of others.

Resolve to be tender with
the young, compassionate
with the aged, sympathetic
with the striving, and tolerant
of the weak and the wrong.
Sometime in life you will
have been all of these.

George Washington Carver (1864–1943)

what is an empath?

An empath is someone who feels what others are feeling at a heightened level. They are incredibly sensitive to atmospheres and vibes and can accurately read emotions. Their talents also extend to reading thoughts, and being able to sense the feelings of plants, animals, and other objects.

Empaths feel more empathy than the average person and are often likened to human sponges, as they absorb the energy of others, both positive and negative. This can lead to health problems, and they often suffer with low moods and fatigue because they are taking on the emotions of those around them.

Empaths easily sense atmospheres and can often walk into a building they have never visited before and recount something of its history. Being highly sensitive also means that empaths react differently to outside stimuli and can become overwhelmed by lots of noise, large crowds, and big personalities.

Empaths around the world

According to a recent survey, around 1–2 per cent of the world's population are empaths. This group includes those who have mirror-touch synesthesia, a condition which means that when another person is being touched, you experience the touch yourself in the same part of your body, or on the opposite side. These "super empaths" can also sometimes feel when another person is in physical pain.

ten ways to tell if you are an empath

There are many benefits to having a heightened sensitivity, and lots of clues to help you identify your gift. You may already be aware if you're an empath, as you will be used to experiencing high levels of emotion and picking up on the pain of others.

your intuition is spot on

You are used to thinking and feeling with your emotions. This is how you connect with others, and it means you are adept at reading your own feelings and sensing when something is right for you. Unlike those who think logically or have a practical nature, you tend to rely on your emotions as a guide, which makes you highly intuitive and more likely to trust gut instincts.

you can find intimacy intimidating

One-to-one relationships might be difficult as you take on your partner's pain and feel things much more deeply. Being extremely sensitive, you find it hard to disconnect and just enjoy your partner's company without absorbing all their feelings. You also need time on your own to regroup, which can be difficult for you to express. Boundaries are essential if you want to have a healthy relationship, but again, this can be difficult to put in place. You hate to upset others because you feel their distress as keenly as they do and because of this, you find arguments extremely stressful, to the point of avoiding confrontation altogether.

you avoid conflict

You are easily hurt by the things that others say. Even throwaway comments can wound you deeply, and a full-blown argument, when the air is charged with anger and emotion, can be too much for your sensitive nature. Your instinct is to make things better, and in the throes of an argument you may be overwhelmed. The urge to run and hide may be strong, because you do not want to put yourself through turmoil.

you are overwhelmed by large crowds

Empaths tend to feel uncomfortable in large groups or crowds. This is because they are highly sensitive and the emotional noise from these gatherings can be too much to take on. You might be able to spend a small amount of time in these situations, but deep down you will be craving alone time to clear your head and heart. You need time to recharge

you need time to recharge

Being an empath can be physically, mentally, and emotionally exhausting. This is because you absorb energy, which can drain you to the core if it's negative. Even positive feelings can overstimulate you, leaving you exhausted and seeking time out. It is important to allow time for your senses to rest.

you mirror the body language of others

A key sign of empathy is to mirror the body language and facial expressions of others. This happens naturally because you are in synch with the other person and feeling what they feel. Many experts in the field of communication suggest consciously mirroring as a technique to connect with others. When we mirror another person, we are saying, "I understand you and I know where you are coming from."

you feel like an outsider

You know that you are unlike other people and you react differently when someone is in pain. This can make you feel like an outsider. Empaths often struggle with loneliness. The key to coping is to find like-minded people and those who understand what you are going through, even if they're not empaths themselves.

you find it hard to set boundaries

Empaths often to struggle to let go and stop feeling,
even when they are on the verge of burnout. Your
instinct is to love and help in any way you can, which
means taking on the energy and pain of others, and
setting boundaries goes against this urge. You may feel
like you would let others down, when in fact it would
help them, because you need time and distance to
recharge and perform effectively.

you see the world in a different way

Empaths find it easy to engage with the world. Your
heightened senses help you see and experience things
fully. You can also pick up on subtle shifts in atmosphere,
so you understand the deeper meaning in any situation.

you are sensitive to sounds and smells

Empaths have highly developed senses which they use
to make sense of the world around them. This means
that you are likely to be sensitive to the sounds and
smells you encounter on a daily basis. You may find that
certain noises or scents trigger an emotional response—
for example, the fragrance of a rose in bloom might
remind you of being a child and playing in the garden,
and this in turn makes you cry with joy.

TRY THIS:

explore your senses

Empathy is a balance between sense and sensitivity, and it starts with you. If you want to be more empathic, you need to look after yourself. Self-care will put you in the right frame of mind to care for others and it will also keep you strong and grounded.

• Consider each sense as an antenna which helps you experience the world at a deeper, more enjoyable level.

• Practice being in the moment and using each sense every day.

• If there is a particular scent you like, or a sound that you love to listen to, then make it a part of your weekly routine.

• Surround yourself with sights, sounds, and smells that you love and revel in the sense of touch and taste. In doing so, you'll develop your empathy and recharge your batteries at the same time.

This exercise will help you learn what makes you feel nourished and energized, and instinctively know when you need to boost positive energy.

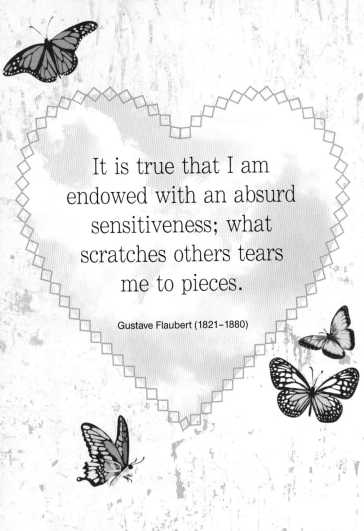

It is true that I am endowed with an absurd sensitiveness; what scratches others tears me to pieces.

Gustave Flaubert (1821–1880)

protection techniques

Whether you are an empath, you have strong empathic tendencies, or you simply want to practice empathy more, it's good to have a handful of practical techniques that you can use to protect yourself. Even if you don't use them all the time, you can draw upon them when you know you are going to be in a situation that could affect your wellbeing.

Each of these tips will help, and with a little preparation, you'll be able to use your gift of empathy freely, without feeling emotionally and physically drained.

learn to say no

Setting boundaries is one of the best ways to protect yourself. If you know that a certain person or situation is going to cause you stress, then limit the amount of time you spend with them. Opt out of situations that you find draining, and suggest other forms of support to those who need your help. Do not be afraid to say no to people. It does not mean you do not care; it simply means you are taking time for self-care.

get back to nature

Nature is an instant mood booster. It's revitalizing, and it
will help to restore strength and energy levels. Being in a
calm and pleasant environment and connecting with the
natural world improve levels of serotonin and oxytocin,
hormones which make you feel good. When you are
feeling low, try taking a mindful stroll through the
countryside. Engage your senses as you walk, and take in
not only what you can see, but what you hear, smell, feel,
and taste. Breathe deeply and let the power of nature
infuse you with vitality.

write and release

Journaling is a great way to shed unwanted emotions.
You can pour your feelings onto the page, which helps
to release them. It is a regular practice that you can get
into the habit of doing at the end of every day, and it
will help to purge your mind and body of negative
energy. If you do not want to keep a regular journal, you
can write your current problems and emotions down
on a piece of paper and then burn it. A physical act,
coupled with the exercise of putting your thoughts and
feelings into words, will help you offload any emotional
residue that you are carrying.

take time out

Do not be afraid to take time out for yourself and schedule in "me time" each week or day as you see fit. Empaths often think they have to carry the world upon their shoulders, but in order to do so, they need to recharge. Find what works for you, and do it, often. Simple things like dipping into your favorite book or TV show, or a long, scented soak in the bath, are just a few ways that you can take time out.

use the power of visualization

If you know you are going to be in a situation that will drain your energy, visualize a protective shield or cloak around you. Imagine its translucent or made of glass, so that you can see through it and connect with others, but you remain protected. This is a powerful tool, as it sends a message to your subconscious to remain detached when engaging with others.

meditate

One of the best tools for empaths is meditation.
A simple breathing meditation that calms the mind
will help you cope with difficult emotions. Set time
aside in your schedule to meditate often, so that it
becomes second nature.

get physical

Exercise is a great way for empaths to de-stress and cast
off the emotions of others. It does not matter what type
of workout you choose; just go for something you enjoy
and that you are able to fully immerse yourself in.
As you work up a sweat, imagine that you're releasing
emotional debris through your pores, and be sure to
spend some time winding down after your session.

BE EMPATHIC: visualization

Visualization can help you connect with others and what they are going through. The next time someone shares their pain with you, try to recreate a picture in your mind of the situation. Imagine it is a framed portrait hanging in a gallery, and watch it grow in size until it becomes a cinema screen. When you can fully see the image, step into it and take their place. Guide yourself through the narrative in your mind, as if you are part of the film, then when you are ready, step out of the picture. Let it reduce in size, until it has completely vanished.

Be kind, for everyone
you meet is fighting
a hard battle.

Anonymous

CHAPTER 2

why is empathy good for us?

the science of empathy

Empathy feels good, whether you are the one who shows it or the one on the receiving end. It creates feelings of closeness and understanding. You feel a sense of belonging—being able to be yourself and having another person see and appreciate what you are going through.

Scientifically, empathy is like flicking a switch. It lights up the brain and triggers dopamine and serotonin, the two key neurochemicals associated with the brain's reward center. This in turn makes us feel good and lifts the mood. It is also hardwired into our DNA and is something that babies understand from day one. When a parent mimics their baby's facial expressions, the baby experiences joy and the part of the brain that deals with emotions fires up. Empathy bonds us together: it stops us feeling isolated in the world and is an important part of our emotional development.

Empathy is the love fire of
sweet remembrance and
shared understanding.

John Eaton (1790–1856)

empathy helps us to feel...

connected

We are no longer on our own: we feel heard and understood, and this in turn helps us feel connected and part of a bigger group, family, or society.

open

We become more open when we connect with others, instead of bottling things up, putting up barriers, and living in isolation. This openness is a two-way thing. When we reach out, we open ourselves up to feel what someone else is feeling.

present

To be empathic, we need to engage with what is going on right now. We need to live in the moment and experience life.

calm

When we no longer feel judged, we relax. There is no need to put on an act, to worry or feel tense. Empathy allows us to feel calm and safe.

accepted

There is no judgment when there is empathy. Our feelings are acknowledged, and we are accepted, just as we are.

self-assured

When someone truly sees and understands us, there's a sense of security and a feeling that we are a valued individual who has something to say and a part to play in society.

creative

When empathy flows between two people, there is an exchange of ideas and feelings. This can spur creativity, allowing both the giver and receiver to feel inspired.

resilient

The more we experience empathy from others, the stronger we become. The sense of connection allows us to grow and feel rooted by our relationships. A secure foundation, which comes from feeling grounded, allows us to face challenges head on.

happy

By experiencing all the benefits on pages 50–51,
we can feel true contentment despite whatever may
be going on around us. Things may go wrong in life, but
when there is empathy, there is support and a light at
the end of the tunnel. Empathy promotes hope.

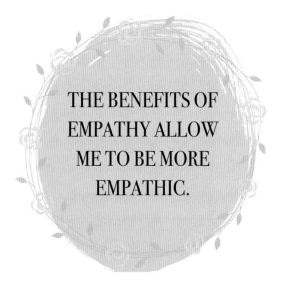

THE BENEFITS OF EMPATHY ALLOW ME TO BE MORE EMPATHIC.

TRY THIS:

use empathic words

Work empathic words into your vocabulary by repeating a different affirmation every day.

• Start with a basic chant, such as "Today I choose to feel…" then pick one of the nine words on pages 50–52 and switch them around on a daily basis.

• To enhance the power of your affirmation, look in the mirror and repeat it several times with feeling.

• Focus on what each word means, and choose an image to go with the chant. For example, if you choose "connected," think about a time when you felt connected with another person and bring an image of that to mind.

• After nine days, begin the process again, and after a month you should notice that it comes naturally and that you genuinely feel the benefits of empathy in your life.

benefits of being empathic

Empathy can transform your world in many ways.

it's good for your health

You might think taking on the emotions of someone else would weigh you down, but the opposite is true. Those who are empathic cope with stress much better than those who struggle to show empathy. Research has proved that when we are empathic, we tend to foster close bonds, which provides a strong and secure base for dealing with daily stress. Those who are able to connect with others and be compassionate also have lower levels of depression and a stronger immune system.

it improves the way you communicate

Those who have learned to see things from another person's perspective naturally find it easier to communicate what they think and feel. They understand where the other person is coming from and have developed techniques to connect with them in a way that will be understood. Empathy helps you become objective. You are more able to see the bigger picture and be flexible in your dealings with others. Because of this, you look at all sides of an argument and are open to what others think.

it improves your relationships

Empathy helps you reach out to others and form social bonds. You share intimacy and learn to accept each other and listen from the heart. All of these factors improve your one-to-one relationships. On a much larger scale, empathy helps create a sense of community. Instead of being obsessed with ourselves, we start to think of others and how we can help them flourish. We become a society that cares for each other.

it's helps to create a positive outlook

When you practice empathy, you naturally feel good. Kindness has its own rewards, and doing something nice for someone because you can feel what they are going through will lift your spirits. You will feel happy that you have helped in some small way, and then it becomes easier to recognize the positives in your own life.

it is contagious

Once you start feeling closer to others, building connections, and opening your heart, you will not be able to stop. The positive energy you create will permeate every part of your life, and you will notice the effects on your mood and the way you think. Life will be less about the struggle, and more about team effort. Soon you'll have started an empathy revolution!

BE EMPATHIC: reconnect with
your memories

Pick a memory that you associate with love. It might be
a moment between parent and child, when you met
your current partner, or something random, such as
watching an animal play. Run through it in your mind and
notice how it makes you feel. If you could associate it
with a color, scent, and sound, what would they be?

Practice opening your heart every day with a mini
meditation to reconnect with this memory. Bring to
mind the memory and the color, scent, and sound
you associated with it. Imagine being surrounded by
the color, inhaling the scent, or immersing yourself
in the sound.

Spending a few moments meditating in this way each
day will relax your heart and mind.

Levels of empathy around the world

According to a 2016 survey, the most empathic country in the world is Ecuador, swiftly followed by Saudi Arabia, Peru, and Denmark. During the survey, participants were asked how happy they felt and how often they helped a stranger or donated time or money to an organization. Personality traits such as agreeableness and conscientiousness were also assessed. The results suggest that countries which favor tight-knit social groups and interdependence appear to be more empathic.

We rise by lifting others.

Robert Ingersoll (1833–1899)

CHAPTER 3

how can we
develop empathy?

the essence
of empathy

When we empathize, we engage with those emotions at a deeper level, and take them upon ourselves. We understand how the other person feels because we feel that way too. Empathy may start with compassion, but it goes much further. To empathize, you must engage your imagination, put yourself in the situation, and let yourself go. There is an amount of risk involved. You cannot keep your guard up or shield yourself from things that might upset you. To truly empathize is to open up, leaving your heart exposed and simply feeling your way forward.

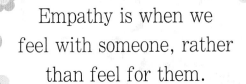

Empathy is when we
feel with someone, rather
than feel for them.

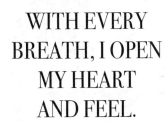

WITH EVERY
BREATH, I OPEN
MY HEART
AND FEEL.

I do not ask the wounded person how he feels; I myself become the wounded person.

Walt Whitman (1819–1892)

open your heart

The heart chakra is the energy center that sits in the middle of your chest. It is from this point that all love flows and you are able to feel and connect with others. You can sense the chakra at work by placing both palms over this area for a few minutes. You should feel a gentle warmth blossom beneath your fingers.

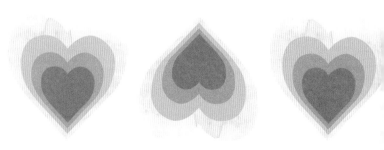

TRY THIS:

opening the heart chakra

This exercise can be done at any point throughout the day when you need to feel, sense, and let love flow.

• Take a moment to calm your mind, and then turn your attention to the center of your chest. Imagine there is a tiny pink rose bud sitting in this space. This perfect flower exudes energy and warmth.

• Every time you inhale, you take in air which feeds the rose.

• Every time you exhale, the petals begin to unfurl, one by one.

• Gradually over the space of a few minutes, the rose begins to blossom, until it is fully open and ready to give and receive love.

• To finish, picture a rosy, pink glow emanating outward from your chest.

choose to care

Scientific research has discovered that empathy is not something we all do naturally or easily. For some people, feeling in this way is a part of their psychological make up, but for others it is an active choice. We can choose to listen to the news report which tells us about the horrific tragedy, or we can switch it off, because we do not want to connect in that way. Every day, we make choices that affect how empathic we are. Sometimes we make those decisions to protect ourselves, and sometimes it is to protect others, because we do not want to misjudge their feelings. Once we understand that empathy is a choice, we can learn to be more empathic every day. When faced with opportunities to empathize, we can take a step back, recognize the choice for what it is, then actively make the decision to engage. It really is that simple.

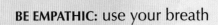

BE EMPATHIC: use your breath

When faced with an opportunity to practice empathy,
take a moment to breathe. Draw the breath from deep
in your belly, and feel it rise into your chest. Hold for
four long beats, then exhale and count for another four
beats. Allow your body to relax, let your shoulders drop
and expand your chest. Take as many calming breaths as
you like, then when you feel ready, make the choice to
engage with the situation.

I choose to connect with
others and share in what
they are feeling.

empathy and body language

You can create empathy using body language and expression. Simple tips and techniques will help you connect with the other person at an emotional level.

eye contact

There's a reason the eyes are called the "windows to the soul." They are our first point of contact when we meet someone new and when we're having a conversation. We can tell so much from someone's eyes. We can see when they are happy, and when they are in pain. The eyes give away the emotions and they are one of the best ways to connect with someone. If you want to be more empathic, adjust your gaze and make sure you maintain eye contact throughout the conversation. This does not mean you have to stare at the person, which could feel intrusive. Gently checking in with the person, and smiling with your eyes, is inviting and will put you both at ease.

posture

A relaxed, open posture is the best stance when trying to be empathic. It gives the impression that you are interested and easy to talk to. When you are relaxed, the person you are with will also feel relaxed. If you feel or look tense, this will come across in the way you stand and present yourself. Be aware of body blocking by crossing your arms or legs, which sends the message that you are closed off and in self-protection mode. Instead stand with your shoulders back and relaxed, softening your chest, and your feet hip width apart.

facial expression

As with your body, keep your facial expression relaxed. Try not to show too much emotion, as this can be off-putting and may put the other person on edge. Be open and friendly. Smile if you feel it is appropriate and sympathize when needed.

mirroring

One of the best ways to connect with another person is to mirror their body language. This is something we do naturally when we are in synch with someone and getting on well. Be aware of what the other person is doing with their body and take your cue from them—so, if they lean a certain way, follow suit. If they open their hands, sit back, or lean forward, do the same.

I stand, move, and act with empathy.

stories and empathy

Stories have been around since the dawn of time. They are the building blocks of society, helping us make sense of the world and everything in it. From those first cave dwellers sitting around the fire and sharing hunting tales, to the tales that developed over time to explain natural phenomena like the sun rising or the changing of the seasons, stories play a key part in our evolution. They help us bond with others and express ourselves, and they can also help us look at the world in new ways, so it makes sense that they are a prominent tool when it comes to building empathy.

When we read or listen to a story, our brain waves slow down and we absorb more information. We relax into the tale and picture it in our mind. Slowly, as we acclimatize to the narrative, we start to imagine ourselves in the same world as the characters. We share in their highs and lows and begin to identify with what they are going through. When we read a story, we cannot help but make it real in our minds, and that helps us experience the emotions of the characters and connect with them at a deeper level.

BE EMPATHIC: imagine the story

When you find yourself in a situation where you want to be more empathic, imagine you are watching a story unfold. Take a step back and look at the characters, including yourself. Take a minute to think about how the story looks for each character, and what they must be thinking and feeling.

TRY THIS:
retell and reshape

- Pick a fairy tale that you know well and reacquaint yourself with the story by reading through it again.

- Once you are familiar with the tale, think about one word that sums up what this story is about—for example, joy, courage, or love.

- Now choose a character from the story and imagine you are retelling the tale from their point of view. Consider the timeline and where they enter the tale, as well as thinking about what they see and how they might view things.

- Put pen to paper and make a few notes or plan out the tale using a storyboard and pictures.

- When you have finished, reread the new narrative and think of a word that sums up this story. Even if you have picked the same word, it is likely that the themes of the story have shifted and it is a different tale, because you have looked at it from a new perspective.

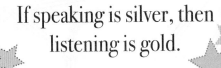

If speaking is silver, then
listening is gold.

Turkish proverb

building empathy through storytelling

The stories we tell ourselves are equally as powerful as the ones we choose to read. We all have subliminal narratives that run through our heads every day. These tales re-enforce the way we think about ourselves and the world around us.

For example, you might start the day with the following narrative: "I'm not looking forward to today, because I have that meeting at work/problem to solve." This story becomes a repetitive loop in your mind, which affects the way you approach everything. It puts you in a bad mood and this is reflected in your actions. By shifting the narrative, you'll look at things from a different perspective. In this example, it might be: "Today is going to be a good day; I'm going to face that meeting and resolve any problems that I face." You will feel more positive, and this will affect your behavior.

We can alter the way we think and learn to look at things from a new perspective by changing our internal dialogue and creating stories that will help us build empathy with others.

BE EMPATHIC: a daily story

Start each day with a simple narrative that focuses on empathy. Imagine you are telling a story—you might begin with something like this: "Today I feel full of empathy. As I take my usual commute into work, I share a smile with a stranger and imagine how they might be feeling. I greet my work colleagues and ask them how they are feeling. I make positive connections with everyone I meet."

Visualize yourself going about your business and imagine the different people you will meet and engage with. Tell yourself that you will use empathy in every interaction and connect with the people in your life on a deeper level.

empathy and mindfulness

Empathy is about feeling what others feel, sharing in their emotions, and understanding what they are going through. There is no judgment, no instant reaction; it is a passive process that happens naturally. Mindfulness is about living in the moment, paying attention, and being present. When we are mindful, we observe, describe, and then act with awareness. Empathy and mindfulness are interlinked, for when we engage with others, we are fully aware of what they are going through. We observe and share in the feelings they are experiencing in that moment.

Studies have shown that those who practice mindfulness, are less self-orientated and more able to identify with the suffering of others. Instead of focusing on goals and self-image, they become more compassionate in the way they communicate, choosing encouragement over criticism and taking the time to really listen when in conversation with others.

how it works

A mindful approach helps to develop an awareness of how you act and react. It also helps you become more conscious of your surroundings. As you get into the habit of being more present, you will find that paying attention to others comes naturally too. You will instinctively sense when someone is in pain because you will be more inclined to stop, observe, and take in what is going on around you. Mindfulness is a stepping-stone to empathy and can help you feel grounded when dealing with the emotions of others.

TRY THIS:

check in with yourself

Make a point of checking in with yourself at least once a day to develop self-awareness and help you feel calm and centered. You can schedule this into your routine by doing it at the same time each day, or just go with the flow and choose a moment that feels right.

• The first step is to stop "actively" doing anything. This can be difficult when we are so used to rushing through the day, but all it takes is a couple of minutes to regroup and connect with ourselves.

• Take a long, deep breath in through your nose and hold the breath for four seconds. As you exhale, let the breath filter from your mouth and count out another four seconds.

• Continue to breathe in this way for a minute to allow your body and mind to settle. You might find it helps to extend the breath by five seconds, and really feel the air fill your lungs and clear your head.

- When you are ready, ask yourself this question: how do I feel right now, in this moment? Do not force an answer; simply let thoughts and emotions flow into and out of your head.

- Pay attention to your body, too, and how you feel physically. If you notice any tension in your muscles, imagine breathing soothing energy into them using the four-second breathing technique.

- Continue to relax and let the feelings ebb and flow. You might also notice other things during this process, such as external sounds and smells or thoughts that crop up out of the blue, but every time something distracts you, gently bring your attention back to your breathing.

- As you come to the end of the exercise, evaluate how you feel once again. Do you feel calmer, open, more energized? Carry this feeling with you into the rest of the day and your interactions with others.

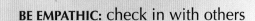

BE EMPATHIC: check in with others

Just as you would check in with yourself at regular points
throughout the day, actively check in with others too.
When you say, "How are you?", ask with genuine interest
and wait for a response. Listen to the words spoken and
trust your intuition. Make an eye-to-eye connection and
look at the person's facial expression and body language.
Get into the habit of asking how someone feels, from
work colleagues to friends and family, and make it
a natural part of your communication.

A kind word is like a spring day.

Russian proverb

empathy and meditation

Meditation has many health benefits, from calming and soothing the mind to improving memory and focus. It helps us deal with stress and shapes our thoughts and behaviors. In addition, it can help us build empathy and act with compassion. Evidence suggests that those who meditate regularly are more likely to feel empathy toward others, because it heightens awareness and enhances our natural ability to look at things from a different perspective.

how it works

Studies suggest that when we meditate, we learn to relate to our emotions in a healthy way. Rather than reacting to negative thoughts or worries, we learn to take a step back, quieten the mind, and not become overwhelmed in the moment. This in turn allows our natural biological resources and caregiving instincts to rise to the surface and guide our actions. Meditation gives us space to breathe. We are no longer consumed with our own fears and concerns, and this allows us to be objective and nurturing toward others.

TRY THIS:
empathy meditation

• Find a quiet spot where you can sit and you will not be disturbed. Make sure you are comfortable and relaxed.

• Close your eyes and focus your attention on your breath. You might want to place both hands beneath your belly and feel the rise and fall as you draw a deep breath in and out.

• Focus on slowing the rhythm of your breathing right down. You can do this by extending each inhalation by a couple of beats.

• Now take a minute to think about empathy. If it was a color, what shade would it be? For example, you might see it as soft and gentle pink, or pure white and bright in hue.

• Imagine that every time you inhale, you are drawing in empathy. See the color streaming through your system, filling your lungs and heart, and filtering to every other part of your body.

• As you exhale, you are releasing fear and anxiety, which allows you to be open and compassionate to others.

• Continue to focus on taking in empathy with every breath. Visualize the color infusing your body and mind and notice how this makes you feel.

• If you find external thoughts drifting into your head, turn your focus back to the rhythm of your breathing.

• To finish, open your eyes and give your body a shake to get the energy flowing.

True empathy requires that you step outside your own emotions to view things entirely from the perspective of the other person.

Anonymous

BE EMPATHIC: when empathy is hard

It can be difficult to be empathic when you are dealing with someone you do not normally get on with. If the person you are faced with upsets or unsettles you, you will automatically put your guard up, and this creates even more of a barrier to communication.

Let empathy win in this situation by taking a couple of deep, meditative breaths. As you inhale, draw empathy into your body, and as you exhale, imagine you're releasing all those pent-up, angry emotions. The influx of oxygen will clear your head and allow some space for you to look at the situation through their eyes.

From caring comes courage.

Lao Tzu (6th century BCE)

your empathy toolkit

There are lots of tools you can use to develop more empathy—small things that can help you open your heart, balance your emotions, and see things from a different perspective. Here are a selection of the best to enhance your empathic skills.

crystals

These semi-precious stones have different properties that can be used for healing and well-being. They can be held, worn, or used as a meditation aid.

moonstone

Moonstone is a lovely, gentle stone that works with the intuition, helping you sense and feel with your emotions. It stimulates the heart chakra, the energy point in the center of your chest and associated with love, and it will help you pick up on the thoughts and feelings of others. Carry or wear the stone close to your heart when dealing with others.

moonstone

rhodonite

A beautiful and loving stone, rhodonite strengthens the spirit and will help you give back to the world by letting love flow. It calms the heart and mind so that you are able to reach out to others from a position of power. It's a stone of unconditional love and compassion and will help you love yourself and others. Rhodonite also makes a great empathic gift for someone who is struggling.

quartz

Quartz is an all-round powerhouse of a crystal. It directs and magnifies the flow of energy and is particularly effective when used in healing. It will give your aura a much-needed boost if you are feeling depleted and will also help you connect with others at a deeper level. Spend five minutes every day holding the crystal in both hands and breathe in the energy.

rhodonite

quartz

essential oils

These scented oils can be burned with a little water in an oil burner, added to bath water, or applied to the skin in a carrier oil.

frankincense

The woody scent of frankincense is known for its uplifting properties. Often used in religious ceremonies, the spicy aroma energizes those who inhale it and enables them to connect with their higher self. It is also thought to be calming and is used as a natural sedative for those who suffer with anxiety. It is ideal for empaths who can be easily overwhelmed and need a fragrance that will boost positive energy.

geranium

The sweet, floral fragrance of geranium soothes the soul and balances the emotions. If you have been going through turmoil or struggling to cope because you have taken on someone else's pain, this stone will help. It restores the spirit and centers you. It is the perfect scent for empaths or anyone who wants to be more empathic in their dealings with others.

rosemary

The strong, astringent scent of rosemary essential oil instantly lifts and brightens the mood. It is a confidence boosting aroma, which can help your feel empowered and strong. In folklore, the herb was used for protection and strength. When you need extra resilience, and to keep negative energy at bay, inhale the scent or add a few drops to your bath water.

herbs

Herbs have powerful medicinal properties, which can help us physically and emotionally. They can be used in teas and tinctures and also added to meals.

lemon balm

Vibrant lemon balm has a zingy, uplifting aroma. A member of the mint family, its leaves have a gentle lemon scent and it is used in a range of medicines. In cooking, it adds fragrant sweetness, and it is a refreshing addition to any herb garden. Used to boost the mood and reduce symptoms of stress, studies have shown that lemon balm also helps with anxiety, making it the perfect choice for those who want to be more empathic and compassionate. It allows you to open your heart to others without absorbing negative energy. Take a handful of fresh leaves and rub them between your fingers to release the scent, then inhale.

lavender

Known for its soothing properties, lavender is a powerful herb, which calms body and mind, balances the emotions, and even helps with insomnia. When used during meditation it promotes a sense of peace and stimulates the heart chakra. Dried lavender is often burned to create a harmonious atmosphere and can instantly lift and balance the emotions. Rub your fingers over the flower head, then inhale, or dab a couple of drops of the oil onto your fingertips and massage into pulse points.

st john's wort

A herbal remedy that has been used for hundreds of years to treat depression, this powerful herb boosts the mood and switches up the mindset. Best used as a tincture or in teas, it will help when you feel weighed down with the emotions of others.

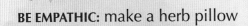

BE EMPATHIC: make a herb pillow

A herb pillow can be carried with you or kept by your bedside to calm and balance your emotions. Take two squares of material that are the same size and sew together three of the edges. Fill the pillow with a mix of mood-enhancing herbs. You can also add a few drops of essential oil to amplify the scent and boost the effects. Sew together the final edge of the pillow and use when you need to center your emotions.

Painkillers

Painkillers can reduce your ability to feel and show empathy. A study carried out in 2013 found that those who took the painkiller acetaminophen (paracetamol) were less likely to feel the pain of others. Researchers believe this is connected to the brain structure and the fact that acetaminophen reduces the "feeling" of pain, which makes you less likely to recognize this in others.

five top tips for
building empathy

practice, practice, practice

Empathy is a skill. It is like a muscle and so it
needs exercising. Regular practice will help your
empathy muscle grow strong and flexible.

go with the flow

Empathy deals with the emotions, so it makes sense
that you should follow your heart. Feel your way in any
situation that requires empathy, and let your emotions
take the lead.

do not judge yourself or others

Empathy is not judgmental. It is about sharing and caring,
whatever the situation. This goes for you, too—do not
judge or berate yourself when you feel you have not
done enough.

be empathic to your own needs

Empathy, like love, starts with you, so be sensitive
to your own needs and emotions.

engage with the world every day

Your senses are like antennae: they can feel the way for
you and help you connect with the world around you.

I use my talents and skills
to help empathy flow.

CHAPTER 4
empathy in action

empathy and you

To truly put yourself in the mind of someone else, you must be prepared to take a step back from who you are. Detach yourself from preconceived ideas and opinions that you have formed over the years, and let your unconditional loving self take over. There is a sense of letting go that comes with empathy; a moment when you must release the past, and all the things that have tainted your soul, and simply be who you are at your purest and most vulnerable. From this point you can slip easily into the mind of someone else, seeing through their eyes and feeling with their heart.

Empathy starts with you, and while you might think there is no need for self-empathy—after all, you know exactly how you feel at any given moment—there is a need to be self-aware: to check in with your feelings and act with self-compassion, to acknowledge your emotions and reach out to yourself in a caring way. This does not mean you revel in the emotions until they consume you. It's about saying, "Yes, I feel this way," then learning to ride the feeling, while being your own best friend. If you can do this, you will also learn to be objective—to experience pain, but also see above and beyond it.

Peace cannot be kept by force; it can only be achieved by understanding.

Albert Einstein (1879–1955)

BE EMPATHIC: be your best friend

Imagine you could split in two when you are experiencing a strong emotion. There is the "you" who is going through the emotion, and the "best friend you" who knows exactly what you are feeling and how to make you feel better. It might sound mind-bending, but no-one knows you like yourself, so have a go.

Imagine stepping out of your body right now and looking at yourself as a separate person. You can still feel your emotion, but you are allowing some space so that you can see the bigger picture and treat yourself with kindness. What do you most need right now? You will instinctively know the answer, and what you need to do to feel better.

ways to show self-empathy

- Give yourself time to feel and do not dismiss your emotions.

- Remind yourself of all the things that make you special.

- Pamper yourself and indulge in some of your favorite things.

- Rest, relax, and breathe.

- Eat healthy, nourishing meals that make you feel good.

- Daydream and let your imagination take over.

- Play and do something just because it is fun.

- Challenge yourself to see the bigger picture.

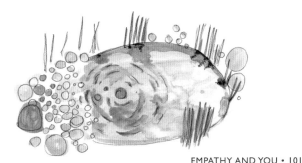

animal friends

Pets are a part of the family, and as such have a close bond with us. We may not share the same language, but we can still communicate and understand each other. The more time we spend together, the more we can tell about them and their general well-being. Just by getting to know their quirks, habits, and the little tell-tale signs that reveal their changing moods, we form a deeper connection, and the empathy between us grows.

Sometimes this empathy is even more potent than the feelings we share with our human family, simply because we try more to understand the animals in our care. We go the extra mile to ensure they are okay and to decipher their body language. We look for the subtle clues that reveal their emotions and they do the same with us. If you are a pet owner, you are sure to have experienced an empathic moment with your animal chum—a time when you were feeling low and they came to your rescue with a lick or a snuggle. Whether you have a cat that does not leave your side when you are feeling anxious, or a dog that rests its head on your lap and fixes you with a loving gaze, the message is clear: "I'm here, and I feel your pain." But why is it that our fur family members are often more empathic than our human tribe?

A study carried out by Animal Cognition investigated the phenomenon of emotional contagion—when one person catches the emotions of another—in canines. The results revealed that dogs react differently to sounds of distress. They know the difference between crying and laughter and respond accordingly by matching the person's behavior. Another study discovered that dogs show empathy to strangers—for example, if they see a person crying, they will offer comfort by nuzzling and licking them. This is something dogs do instinctively when they mirror their owners. Being in synch in this way means they are able to pick up on fears, moods, and heightened emotional states.

Cats are harder to read than their canine counterparts and have a reputation for being independent, but they also tap into their owners' emotions and display empathy. They do this by reading facial expressions and sensing subtle changes through their highly honed sense of smell. While they might not mirror us like dogs, they show their emotions through body language and visual clues, such as the long, slow blink, which means "I love you," and the head butt, which basically says, "I'm here, and I'm with you."

Like humans, some animals will be more empathic than others, depending on their background, personality, and the bond that you share with them, but the evidence is clear—our pets really do care and want to share in our pain and our happiness.

BE EMPATHIC: connect with your pet

A loving gaze crosses the boundaries between species and speaks volumes. Couple this with a powerful subliminal message of love and you are sure to make an empathic connection with your animal friend. The next time you are in your pet's company and sharing a quiet moment, gaze softly into their eyes and speak a message of your fondness for them in your mind. Imagine the feeling pouring directly from your heart into theirs.

I USE BODY LANGUAGE TO COMMUNICATE MY LOVE, EMPATHY, AND COMPASSION.

ways to show empathy with pets

- Make time for your pet and get to know them through play and stroking.

- Talk to your pet using a soothing tone to reassure and comfort them.

- Give them treats and make a fuss of them. It's important to let your animal family know how much they mean to you.

The power of pets

Studies have found that pet owners have higher levels of empathy than non-pet owners. Research also suggests that children with pets tend to be more prosocial and empathic. It is thought that owning a pet teaches emotional intelligence and the ability to understand and connect with others.

• Do not shout at them if they show signs of bad behavior; instead, take a step back and consider why they are acting out and if they are trying to get your attention for another reason.

• Mirror their body language, with head butts and rubs, so that they know you accept them on their level.

• Learn as much as you can about the way they communicate, so that you can understand when they need love and when they need space.

It is a man's sympathy with
all creatures that truly makes him
a man. Until he extends his circle
of compassion to all living things,
man himself will not find peace.

Albert Schweitzer (1875–1965)

family ties

Your family know you better than anyone, and the feeling is mutual. You are connected by bonds which go much deeper than everyday communications and you have shared experiences that bring you even closer. It makes sense that empathy would come naturally with family members, although this is not a given. Rifts and breakdowns in communication are a part of family life and can make it harder for you to connect with and understand your nearest and dearest.

A recent study into the genetic roots of empathy has shown that around 10 per cent of the variation in empathy between people is down to their genes, so while we can learn to be more empathic, a degree of how empathic we are is inherited in our biological makeup. Empathy is a key family value and it can be nurtured. It helps parents provide a caring environment for their children to live in, and it motivates children to act with empathy and see things from a different perspective.

BE EMPATHIC: family bonding time

Spending time together will help you bond and better understand family members. Get into the habit of having regular family get-togethers. These can be simple gatherings over coffee and cake, or days out, where you experience something new together. If you have a large family, take it in turn to plan events and outings, so that everyone gets a chance to do something they enjoy. Use these get-togethers as an opportunity to talk and check in with family members. Even if relationships are strained, when you spend time doing something fun together, you will find a common ground from which you can reconnect and learn to see each other's point of view.

ways to show empathy with family

- Allow everyone to have their say and express how they feel.

- If there is a problem, resist the urge to blame, and instead take a deep breath and some time out.

- Get to know your older relatives by asking questions and learning about their life.

- Volunteer your time and offer to help with any chores around the home or garden.

- Share special memories of times you have shared together and enjoy reliving the feelings associated with them.

• Take it in turns to tell each member of your family how much they mean to you and why you love them.

• Get creative and express your love for your family by doing something arty, such as writing a poem or drawing a picture.

• Delve into family history and learn about your ancestral roots.

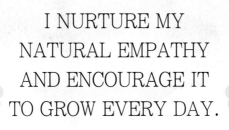

I NURTURE MY
NATURAL EMPATHY
AND ENCOURAGE IT
TO GROW EVERY DAY.

the empathy of friendship

Your friends are the family you choose. They are the people who "get" you; the ones you turn to in times of crisis as well as when you need to have fun. They are your tribe and as such they know you better than most. It is a two-way relationship and just as they are there for you, you are there for them. Some friendships last a lifetime—they are built for all the highs and the lows—while others are transient and come and go when you need them. Whatever types of friendship you have, they all require an amount of empathy to survive. It is the common thread that ties people together and it will help you through the roughest times.

Empathy and technology

Technology facilitates empathy. Research has shown that the development of the internet and social media can have a positive effect on empathy, as it means we are able to reach out to our friends and those who need help, even if we live further afield.

TRY THIS:

gratitude list

• Start a list with the words, "I am grateful for you, because…" and then write down at least five things that make them extra special to you.

• Now that you have the list in front of you, use it to reach out to your friend, whether face to face, on the phone, or via a video call, email, or text message. The important part is that you thank the person for being in your life and tell them why you are grateful. Open your heart and reach out to them, and they will return the favor.

Practicing heartfelt communication like this will improve your relationship and help you connect with each other at a deeper level. You will be more likely to show empathy and compassion and to receive it.

BE EMPATHIC: learn from your friends

Think of a time when a friend showed you empathy.
Bring to mind the situation, then consider how they
acted. Did they show their compassion with words or
actions? How did it make you feel?

Now consider the friendship that you have and think of
a time when you were empathic with them. What did
you do to show your empathy? If you are struggling to
think of an example, ask yourself why, and then consider
how you could be more empathic. Make a list of things
you could do in the future that would show empathy
and compassion.

I AM GRATEFUL FOR THE
EMPATHY I RECEIVE.

ways to show empathy with friends

- Listen, listen, listen, and then listen some more.

- Share words of encouragement and make sure
  you tell them how much they mean to you.

- Do something that makes you both laugh, such as
watching your favorite comedy or sharing your best jokes.

- If you cannot catch up with them in person,
  check in regularly by phone or video call.

- Write a letter of thanks for your friendship with them.

- Share a new experience together—even something
  simple such as going for a walk somewhere new.

- Give them flowers to show how much they mean to you.

- When they are feeling under the weather,
  cook them a meal.

empathy at work

According to research, empathy and compassion are essential components within the workplace, and contribute to a more productive environment. When we show empathy toward our colleagues, we are saying, "I understand where you are coming from," and this is the glue that cements healthy working relationships. Acts of compassion among colleagues help to boost morale and have a positive impact on performance culture, which in turn creates a more harmonious working environment.

At management level, empathy is cited as one of the key attributes required by leaders, as it helps them better understand their employees. Managers who show empathy are more likely to listen to members of staff and foster a supportive team environment.

take a minute...

We all experience difficult relationships and differences of opinion, and at work we are more likely to come across people who think and act differently from ourselves. It is easy to judge and form preconceived ideas, which then affects working relationships. Instead of jumping to conclusions or reacting without thought when you disagree with someone, take a minute to see things from their perspective.

• Take a step back, physically and mentally.

• Take a deep breath and count to ten, then refocus your mind by asking, "Why do they feel/act this way? What is really going on?"

• Trust your gut when it comes to the answers. If you feel that there is something deeper going on, then tread gently and give them space to work it out.

TRY THIS:

write it out

If you're struggling to show empathy toward a work colleague, try this simple exercise to work through any blocks. It's best to carry this out at home or away from your desk where you are likely to be influenced by negative emotions. You will need a pen and some sheets of paper.

• Find a quiet place where you will not be disturbed. You may also like to burn some geranium scented oil to balance your emotions and promote clear thought.

• Start by bringing your colleague to mind. Picture them in the working environment and notice what emotions surface as you do this: you might feel frustrated, angry, or confused. Let these emotions settle, then take your pen and begin to write down how you feel.

• Outline why you feel this way, and if you have a particular grievance, write this down, too.

• Put the paper to one side and take a few calming breaths.

• Now picture the person again and imagine stepping into their shoes. Try and see things from their perspective and notice how you feel. You might experience other emotions, but let them flow through you.

• When you are ready, take another sheet of paper and write as if you are the other person. Explain how you feel and why you feel this way. Let your emotions fill the page, then when you have finished, put it with the other sheet.

• Take a few more calming breaths. To finish, take one more sheet of paper and write down a positive statement, such as, "I am open to moving forward and connecting with you on a deeper level. I let my empathy flow."

If you judge people, you have no time to love them.

Anonymous

BE EMPATHIC: it's the little things

A kind word, a smile, a small gift, or a favor are all ways that you can show someone you care. When we reach out in this way to someone, they are more likely to let us in, and so begins an empathic relationship.

At work, you have the opportunity to show your empathy in many different ways. A carefully timed offer of assistance with something on their to-do list, a small gesture of making a drink for someone who is obviously stressed, or just a few words of encouragement will make all the difference.

ways to show empathy at work

- Stop speaking and start listening.

- Get to know your colleagues by asking questions.

- When you have spare time, ask them if they need help with anything.

- Go for lunch together.

- Set yourself a team challenge and work together to achieve it.

- Bake a cake and bring it in for everyone to enjoy.

- Be there, be present, and be aware.

- Accept your differences and learn to appreciate them.

caring for the community

We are social beings, and we are hardwired to mingle, to get to know each other and form bonds. The mirror neurons in our brains motivate us to engage with others and to empathize with them. This is inherent to who we are, but it is also affected by other factors, such as the way in which we relate as a society. Changes to the way we connect and communicate affect our interpersonal relationships. We are less likely to call someone to wish them well when we can post online instead. We use the internet to connect with people around the world, but we may well not know our neighbors or the community that we live in. This disconnection with what is going on in our immediate environs affects the way we think and feel. It makes us less likely to share and care, and fosters an atmosphere of indifference and, in some cases, hate for what we do not know or understand. Empathy is the answer. It is the way to bring people together and to build a thriving community that has care at its core.

Empathy and young people

Empathy Day was created in 2017 to drive the empathy movement forwards and introduce young people to the importance of being empathic. It usually falls on or around June 10. Through the use of books and stories, children are encouraged to see things through the eyes of the characters as a way of helping empathize with others.

Empathy Week is a global schools program, which usually falls in mid- to late February. A range of schools from different countries take part in carefully coordinated activities, using the power of film to promote empathy, understanding, and leadership skills in young people.

BE EMPATHIC: connect to your roots

Find out about your local area. Even if you have not lived there long or you were not born there, you still have ties to the place where you chose to set down roots. Do some digging and look into the history. What was it like to live there a hundred years ago? How has it developed and changed? Research who in the community has lived there the longest. What can they tell you about the place and the changes that they have witnessed?

Imagine you are a detective, piecing together clues about the place where you live and the type of people who live there. This will help you build a bigger picture and also develop empathy for your community.

TRY THIS:
storytelling circle

Storytelling is something that happens naturally when you get a group of people together. It is a form of communication and an easy way to bond with and get to know those you live with in the community. You do not have to create an official storytelling club, unless you want to; simply invite some of the people that you know to a gathering with their favorite drinks and nibbles and let the stories come.

• To promote the natural flow of tales, sit people in a semicircle so that everyone can see and speak to each other.

• If you want to give the group a theme—for example, stories about your home or local tales—then do so, otherwise just ask people to share their memories.

• Encourage everyone to take a turn, even for just a couple of minutes. To help those who are struggling, prepare a few questions as prompts and invite other group members to ask questions, too.

• Make it fun. Storytelling is a way of making sense of the world and some of the things that happen to us, but it can also be incredibly emotional, depending on the subject matter, so be open and ready to listen. Show your support and love when needed.

ways to show empathy in the community

- Say hello to people that you see on the street.

- Start up a conversation with someone who lives on your street or in your building

- Make a point of getting to know one new person a month: that means really taking an interest in who they are and their likes and interests.

- Start a community group.

- Host a fundraising event.

- Check in with your neighbors and ask if they need help.

- Offer to shop for the elderly or vulnerable.

- Champion a local cause, like litter picking or recycling.

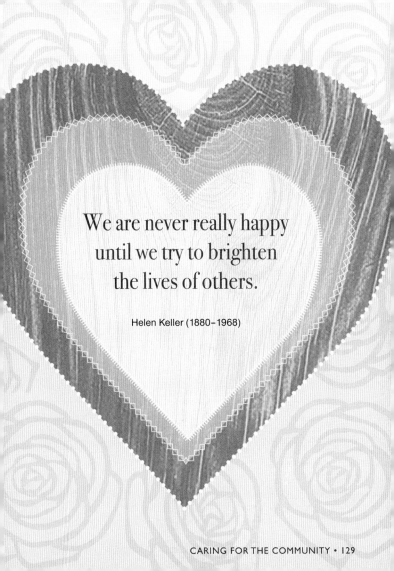

We are never really happy
until we try to brighten
the lives of others.

Helen Keller (1880–1968)

the empathy of nature

Nature is a great teacher and offers examples of empathy at every turn, from the gifts of each season which are freely given to the way the ecosystem supports the environment and the wildlife. The soil sustains and provides new growth. The plants and shrubs become a source of nourishment to all manner of creatures, and the trees support us by providing oxygen, protection, and materials that we can use to survive. Trees also reach out to each other with a complex underground network of roots, which allows them to communicate and share nutrients with other trees in their wood.

All of nature is interlinked and works seamlessly for the welfare of each other. Animals use their super senses to sniff out pain and fear. They also sense the subtle shifts in atmosphere and energy and work with them, knowing when to retreat and recharge and when to rebuild and reproduce. The symbiotic relationships within the natural world keep everything ticking along nicely. Nothing is redundant or left behind; everything and everyone has a supportive role to play and can offer something to the picture. Yes, there are times of conflict and destruction, but they are always followed by a period of renewal, as nature works together to rejuvenate and reinvent itself.

We, too, are a part of this. We are born from nature, and we have an empathy with the natural world, which is instinctive, and a part of our make-up. How we relate to our surroundings and what we do to help the environment are acts of empathy. Even small things, like planting a flower or feeding the birds, have an impact and show that we care. They illustrate, without words, that we understand and appreciate the world around us and that we want to play our part.

BE EMPATHIC: listen to nature

Think of nature as a friend, a person you can walk with.
Spend time in her company by going for long walks in
the park or the countryside or simply by being in your
own back garden. Learn about the natural world by
reading books and listening to others. Open your heart
to nature, just as you would another human being.
Reach out with a gentle touch and ask, "What can
I do to help you?" You will find that inspiration comes
when you take the time to listen to nature and
breathe in your environment.

TRY THIS:

go wild with nature

- If it's possible and easy for you, designate a small square of your garden or allotment to be wild. Let the grass grow, let the wildflowers bloom, and simply watch nature take its course.

- If you want to encourage new growth, you could sow some wildflower seeds and sprinkle them regularly with water.

- Ask yourself what else you can do to help nature flourish. You might want to include a compost patch for the insects and worms or make some space for other small animals to find their home.

- Make a point of checking in with this space every so often and notice how it changes.

ways to show empathy in nature

There are many other simple ways to connect with nature and show you care.

- Go on a mindful nature walk.

- Plant a tree in your garden.

- Put up a bee box.

- Feed the birds

- Volunteer to pick up litter in the park.

- Take on an allotment and plant some vegetables.

- Learn about nature.

- Go bird watching.

- Make a bug hotel.

- Clear thoroughfares for hedgehogs.

- Reduce your waste.

- Eat sustainably.

the flower of empathy

Sow the seeds of empathy wherever you go. Scatter them far and wide, over moist fertile soil but also coarser terrain. Let them find their place to take root in the earth. Water them daily, with a few drops of encouragement and a sprinkling of kindness. Let them bathe in the light and warmth of the sun's rays. Then slowly, steadily, watch as they grow, getting stronger day by day. Should any weeds grow with them, root them out before they have chance to settle and strangle any saplings. Give them air and room to stretch and find their way. Let them dance among the gentle breeze and test the fluid power of their strength and flexibility. Then, when they are ready, sit back and watch them bloom. Most of all, enjoy and share their beauty with the rest of the world.

I CONNECT WITH THE EMPATHY OF NATURE AND UNDERSTAND MY ROLE IN THE WORLD.

empathy in folklore

Folklore is a body of culture, which encompasses traditional stories, beliefs, and customs, and is recognized by different groups of people to represent who they are and how they came to be. Gathered over time, folklore connects people to their past and helps them make sense of their place in the world. Usually through the power of myth and legend, this lore is passed down and used to instill morals and behaviors.

Empathy is a key part of folklore, as it unites groups of people and helps them understand the deeper meaning which connects them. Many of the tales and beliefs which crop up in folklore from around the world feature characters with high levels of empathy and display a more empathic way of being together. For our ancestors, empathy was the glue that kept them close and gave their lives meaning.

TRY THIS:

get your folklore fix

• Choose a mythology that you are interested in and gather together a selection of tales and beliefs. Even if you are not a fan of myth and legend, there may be tales or local customs that have always fascinated you.

• Do some digging and find out what is at the heart of these tales. Read the stories and summarize the key themes within the tales and why the characters act in certain ways.

• What are the main lessons and are there any instances of empathy? You will soon begin to see that empathy is the cornerstone of existence and is key to evolution and progress.

goddess of empathy

Kuan Yin, also known as Guan Yin and Quan Yin, is the beautiful Buddhist goddess of compassion. Associated with empathy and mercy, her name means "she who hears the cries of the world." A symbol of kindness and purity, this serene deity was thought to have attained enlightenment after many years of meditation and study, but gave up on the blissful state of nirvana when she heard the painful cries of those still suffering in the world. She believed it was her responsibility to be there and to care for those in need, sharing in their woes and offering her support. Often depicted in white flowing robes and sitting on or near a lotus flower, Kuan Yin is thought to be the physical representation of empathy and compassion.

The recipe for empathy is simple: kindness mixed with compassion, plus equal parts open heart and mind.

BE EMPATHIC: inspired by the divine

Let the beautiful Buddhist deity Kuan Yin inspire you to be more empathic. When you see someone struggling or having a bad day, lend an ear or a hand instead of walking away. Offer your help in any way that you can; even if it is unwanted, at least you have reached out to them and shown that others care and want to share in what they are feeling.

If I can stop one heart
from breaking, I shall not
live in vain.

Emily Dickinson (1830–1886)

I am empathy

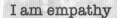

I exist, but you cannot see me.

I slip between words and feelings.

When you smile, I might be at the back of your mind.

When you cry, I can offer my healing.

I help you connect with the ones you love.

I help you make friends with strangers.

I am there when you need me to forge a bridge.

When all hope is lost, I'm the savior.

Some know me better than others,

And some hardly know me at all.

Most seek an audience now and then,

But some always come when I call.

I have no name, that was given to me,

Only a term and a concept.

I am the one that everyone seeks

And the one you will never forget.

I exist but you cannot see me.

I'm the breath between words and feeling.

In the blink of an eye, I can open your heart.

In this world, I can offer true meaning.

acknowledgments

I would like to thank my wonderful editor Carmel Edmonds and the team at CICO Books for helping to create such a beautiful and uplifting book.

I would like to say a big thank you to my mum and dad, for showing me the true meaning of empathy and helping to nurture this quality in me from a young age. Also, thank you to my gorgeous fur family, Minnie, Honey, Ziggy, and Diego: you are more than feline friends, you are masters of mindfulness and empathy. I have learned so much simply sharing my life and home with you.

picture credits

Artworks are by Amy Louise Evans © CICO Books unless otherwise stated below.

pp. 9, 14, 28, 44, 47, 56, 61, 69, 73, 77, 82, 86, 87, 93, 97, 100, 105, 111, 116, 122, 126, 129, 130, 132, 139 by Jenny McCabe © CICO Books

pp. 3, 32, 33, 40, 41, 42, 117, 124, 128, 135 © Nastya Vaulina/Shutterstock.com

pp. 2, 4, 5, 39, 142, 143 © tsupong/Shutterstock.com

pp. 14, 28, 44, 56, 69, 73, 77, 82, 86, 93, 100, 105, 111, 116, 122, 126, 132, 139 © TairA/Shutterstock.com

p. 15 © Lara Cold/Shutterstock.com